FOUR
WHEELING

FOUR
WHEELING

BY JOHN D. FARQUHAR

BILL HOLDER

GARY WESCOTT,
The Turtle Expedition, Unltd.

Photography by John D. Farquhar
Gary and Monika Wescott

Foreword by Gary Wescott,
The Turtle Expedition, Unltd.

COURAGE BOOKS

9 8 7 6 5 4 3 2 1

Digit on the right indicates the number of this printing.

Library of Congress Cataloging-in-Publication Number
93-085544

ISBN 1-56138-400-3

Printed in Slovenia

First published by Courage Books, an imprint of
Running Press Book Publishers
125 South Twenty-second Street
Philadelphia, Pennsylvania 19103

PAGE 1: *A Jeep CJ5 in a wheelie at the All Four Fun Weekend in Colorado.*

PAGES 2-3: *Four wheeling among the red rock spires and pinnacles near Moab, Utah.*

BELOW: *Camel Trophy competitors haul a Range Rover out of the mud in Madagascar in 1987. Held in a different location every year, the Camel Trophy pits four wheelers against some of the most hostile terrain in the world.*

BELOW RIGHT: *A four wheeler meets one of man's oldest forms of transportation in Oaxaca, Mexico.*

CONTENTS

FOREWORD

Four wheeling is many things to different people. From desert racing in Mexico to the World Class Wha-Hoo Jeeping on the boulder-strewn mining trails of Northern California's Sierra Nevada mountains or the Colorado Rockies; from the international jungle adventures of events such as the Camel Trophy to the chrome and glitz of monster show trucks with mega-horsepower engines; from the excitement of sand drags, hill climbs and mud bogs to the freedom and adventure of overland expeditions; this book covers them all.

The reader will be both entertained and educated by the variety of facets international four wheeling has taken. The text reflects insights of journalists who have spent years writing for many of the world's leading four wheel drive publications. The bonanza of images has been selected from the files of some of the most experienced photographers in the field. If a picture is worth a thousand words, then certainly, there are volumes represented here. For both the novice and the confirmed 4×4 aficionado, a wealth of information awaits you within these pages.

Gary Wescott
The Turtle Expedition, Unltd.
Writer, Photographer, Producer,
Editor-at-Large FOUR WHEELER Magazine

INTRODUCTION

In the spring of 1993, the German auto manufacturer Mercedes Benz announced that the company would build a new automotive plant in the United States, with ground-breaking in the spring of 1994. In this age of car companies constantly reporting losses or only small gains, why would one of the world's giants want to build a new multimillion dollar facility? The answer is that Mercedes wishes to cash in on the hottest segment of motor vehicles – the light sport four wheel drive utility vehicle. Four wheeling, and four wheel drive vehicles, have taken America, and many other parts of the world, by storm.

Chrysler-Jeep, already hard-pressed to fill domestic orders, has been asked to double production of right-hand drive vehicles for sales in the United Kingdom. Sales in four wheel drive vehicles have steadily grown to the point that they are cutting into other markets. The other markets have answered the challenge by offering four wheel drive as an option on some models – an example is the Ford Aerostar, which offers an electric four wheel drive option.

Today's marketplace in the United States offers more than 50 production models of four wheelers. Domestic offerings range from the Jeep Wrangler to the civilian Hum-Vee, and the imports from the Suzuki Samurai to the Range Rover (built by Land Rover). Many car lines offer a four wheel drive option, usually sold as "all wheel drive," along with the old standby Subaru that has produced four wheel drive automobiles for years.

Four wheelers serve from everyday activities such as getting the kids to school and loading up with groceries to adventurous ones such as mountain rescue and exploration. Yet experts calculate that less than five percent of the four wheelers sold will ever be used offroad. And many

BELOW: *The 1994 Defender is the newest Land Rover model to be introduced in North America.*

ABOVE: *A Jeep Renegade takes to the hills in Utah.*

RIGHT: *This four wheeler is airborne on a stretch of the Baja 1000, one of several long-distance cross country races in which 4×4s compete.*

owners will seldom use the four wheeler with all four locked in, even when conditions warrant it. While it is easy to understand why the farmer or the offroad enthusiast needs four wheel drive, why does it seem that so many others are purchasing these vehicles?

When four wheelers are mentioned, many think of stories of high adventure and excitement. A family station wagon has none of the glamour value of a 4WD. The 4×4s have become quite the vogue of the 1990s, and it seems that they will stay in fashion for a long time to come, for, more than anything else, they offer something that few other vehicles offer – assurance. Four wheelers never seem to slip and slide; they move through rain and snow as though they were on a dry road.

Beyond the fashionable and the trend setters, are the true 4WD enthusiasts – those who see Jeeps, Blazers, Land Rovers, and Broncos for what they were truly built for: offroad excitement. From the trail riders who challenge the toughest trails that Mother Nature can offer and those who use 4×4s to travel across entire continents, to those who seek the contests of speed, strength, and endurance offered by the sleek sand dragsters and the deep and dirty world of mud bogging, there is a world of adventurers who truly put their vehicles to every test. For the creative, the four wheel drive show circuit offers an outlet. For the real showman,

ABOVE: *Four wheelers enjoy seeking out challenging trails and exploring unknown territory.*

LEFT: *Expedition 4×4s can carry intrepid travelers to remote parts of the earth, such as Bolivia.*

9

the true giants of the four wheeling world are the monster trucks. In these different aspects of four wheeling there are no lines drawn; they often cross over, and blend together. Show trucks can show up on the trail, and boggers sometimes race on the sand.

Four wheeling has become organized, with four wheel drive clubs and associations both on the national level and on the regional level in the United States. Some of the associations sanction competitive events, others promote offroad use, and some are involved in all aspects of four wheeling. One of the largest regional groups in the United States is the East Coast Four Wheel Drive Association. They are active in 11 states, with 62 member clubs and nearly 1700 members active in all types of four wheeling. They participate in all aspects of four wheeling, from trail riding and competitive events to public services such as transportation in weather emergencies to trail cleanup in parks and reserves.

Four wheeling offers something for everyone, so ease back and enjoy this trip into four wheeling.

ABOVE AND RIGHT: *Four wheelers can compete in exciting offroad competitions, such as hill climbs.*

FAR RIGHT AND OPPOSITE: *Whether going solo or with a group, four wheeling can take you nearly anywhere. Such organizations as Tread Lightly! encourage enthusiasts to respect the environment while enjoying access to out-of-the-way places.*

FROM THEN TO NOW

BY

JOHN D. FARQUHAR

ABOVE: *The military "Mutt" was designed for air drops in the Vietnam War. It was lightweight, with an aluminum frame and body.*

RIGHT: *The four-cylinder engine of an original Ford GPW of World War II.*

Today's interest in four wheel drive vehicles can be traced to its origins in the days of World War II. Prior to the war, the U.S. military deemed that the horse was no longer a viable option on the modern battlefield. But the need still existed for something light and fast to perform patrols and move supplies and men to the front. The first prototype vehicle was designed and fabricated in less than two months by Karl K. Probst, then Chief Engineer at the American Bantam Car Company. This was the forerunner of today's Jeep. In all, the Bantam BRC-40 only totalled around 2600 production units, and very few still exist today. Most were shipped to Great Britain and Russia for the war.

Improvements in the vehicle design were performed by Ford, The General Purpose (GP), and Willys-Overland, the Quad. The U.S. Army chose the Willys, and designated it the MB. To help boost

ABOVE: *Down to the last bolt, an original World War II vintage Ford GPW. The Ford and Willys MB were the grandfathers of today's 4×4s.*

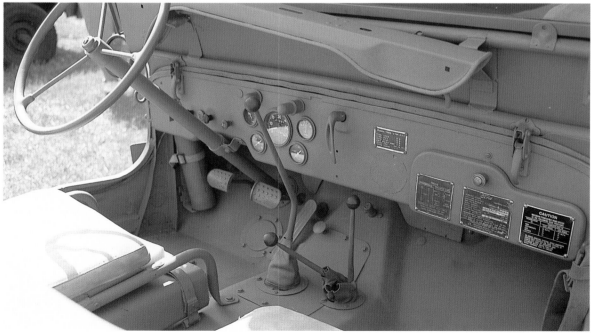

LEFT: *The interior of the Ford GPW was quite spartan when compared with today's 4×4s.*

production, Ford was also awarded production contracts. The Ford model was the GPW (General Purpose-Willys). The name Jeep was not official, but a nickname. It is thought that the name was either from a long pronunciation of the letters "GP," or based on a Popeye cartoon character of the era known as "Jeep," who could go anywhere and do anything. Seeing the commercial advantages after the war, Willys soon gained copyright to the name Jeep.

With 350,000 built for the war, the Jeep quickly won the hearts of the GIs, as it was the only vehicle that could move when everything else got stuck. The MBs brought the GIs their mail and supplies, and carried the wounded back to the aid stations. A British SAS Major, David Sterling, first saw the Jeep in 1942, and recognized its potential as an offensive vehicle. He had machine guns mounted on them, and conducted raids on German airfields deep behind the lines. This type of action and similar adventures added to the plucky little four wheeler's legend.

In 1945 the war ended, and Willys introduced

ABOVE: *A restored 1972 Land Rover, formerly used by the British Army.*

RIGHT: *A late 1940s model CJ2A awaits overhaul and restoration.*

OPPOSITE TOP: *A typical CJ5, ready to take to the trails.*

OPPOSITE BOTTOM: *A 1953 Willys pickup truck in mint condition. Owned by John Reigel of Farmersville, Ohio, the 40-year-old truck has less than 40,000 miles on the clock.*

the civilian CJ2A, producing over 100,000 over four years. In 1949 the CJ3A was introduced, and in 1953 the CJ3B debuted. On the military side, the M38A1 was produced in 1952, which led to the CJ5 in 1955. The CJ5 stayed in production for nearly 30 years. There were two other models of the classic Jeep built: the CJ6 and CJ7, which were different in wheelbase and powerplants. There were other vehicles that also carried the Jeep name: the Beachwagon, pickup, and Commando, all in four wheel drive. Two models that carried the Jeep logo that were not four wheel drive were the Jeepster and the familiar postal Jeep. Meanwhile, other American car companies picked up on the trend, with Ford and GM offering 4WD trucks.

One of the things that kept early four wheelers down on the farm or out in the country was the fact that they were rather spartan. They were noisy, the ride was rough, and the vehicles were a bit ungainly. But as Americans became more recreationally minded, and wanted or needed larger, more powerful, and more comfortable four wheelers to tow boats and travel trailers, the manufacturers

ABOVE: *A late 1960s Jeep Commando restored to showroom shape, but still following the call of the trail.*

RIGHT: *The full-size Jeep Grand Wagoneer was introduced in 1962. The Jeep wagons changed little in their first 20 years of production.*

responded. Kaiser-Willys (formerly GPW) introduced the Jeep Wagoneer in 1962. Chevy responded with the Suburban, which still leads the pack in room, ride, and power. Over the years, the custom Suburban has become such a hit in Texas that it has been dubbed the "Texas Cadillac." Chevrolet also offed the Blazer, and Ford entered the race with the Bronco. International did quite a business with the Scout and Travelall models, until the company left the consumer market. But as the vehicles grew in size and comfort they became less usable offroad, and the Jeep remained king with the offroad crowd.

In the 1970s a new 4WD vehicle appeared: the light quarter-ton pickup. At first most of these were Toyota and Datsun imports, but soon American trucks appeared and sales went through the roof. All the major manufacturers soon got the idea to scale down the big utility wagons. Jeep introduced new versions of the Cherokee and Wagoneer wagons, which were smaller, more comfortable, more fuel efficient and still offroad tough. Ford designed a smaller version of the Bronco, the Bronco II. The Jimmy and S10 Blazer were General Motors' new lightweights. The market was further

crowded by imports, from Nissan, Toyota, Suzuki, Land Rover, and others.

Complaints were heard from the dyed-in-the-wool four wheelers that the new vehicles were too streamlined and soft for any serious offroad use. But the new breed of 4×4s soon proved they were as nimble as the older models, and in many cases, thanks to their smaller size, could go places that the older, larger four wheelers couldn't. In 1986 the long line of Jeep CJs ended with the introduction of the Wrangler, which features a lower center of gravity, a smoother ride, and a sleeker look. To many, the new Jeep seems to resemble the original CJ2A more than any of the later models.

To give the reader an idea of what today's four wheelers offer, here is a profile of the Chrysler-Jeep Grand Cherokee, introduced in 1992. This new wagon is designed with unibody construction, rather than the traditional frame, making it stiffer and giving it a more car-like ride. The standard powerplant is 4. liter six, and a 5.2 liter V8 is optional. Three different four wheel drive driveline optionals are offered. Although a five-speed manual transmission is standard, over 90 percent of the buyers are choosing the four-speed automatic. It

BELOW: *The GMC Suburban has been used since the 1960s for both work and play. Considered one of the best recreation towing vehicles, it has been offered in various models, and in both two- and four wheel drive versions.*

RIGHT: *The extremely popular Ford Explorer, one of the new breed of 4×4 light sport wagons. It offers the comfort of a car, the room of a mini-van, and the toughness of a 4×4.*

BELOW: *Perhaps the best appointed production 4×4, the Chrysler-Jeep Grand Cherokee, introduced in 1992.*

LEFT: *The Jeep Wrangler was introduced to replace the long line of CJs that ceased production in the 1980s. With its lower body stance and flat fenders, it looks similar to the Willys MB.*

BELOW: *The Nissan Pathfinder is one of the leading Japanese imports in the U.S. market.*

comes with airbag, cruise control, A/C, fuel injection, and other amenities. The interior has the luxury of a towncar, but considering the $20,000 to $30,000 price tag, it is doubtful that consumers would settle for less.

On the military side, after nearly a half-century of service, the Army quietly retired the Jeep from active duty in the early 1980s. It was replaced by the High Mobility Multi-Purpose Wheeled Vehicle (HMMWV), nicknamed the Hum-Vee, and built by AM General. Despite a rough start, the Hum-Vee has proven itself capable of replacing the old warhorse. Following its popularity during the Persian Gulf War, a civilian version has been introduced. In civilian issue it is called the Hummer, and is powered by a General Motors 6.2 liter diesel engine, and three-speed automatic transmission. Although streetworthy, it does not offer the comfort of the other 4WD wagons. It is a solidly built backcountry offroad machine, and will go places that no other production 4×4 can. The Hummer's sticker price of over $40,000 will prevent it from becoming a common sight at the shopping mall.

At the other end of the spectrum, nearly everyone has seen the ads on how to acquire a military surplus Jeep for as little as $44.95. In fact, the U.S. government has sold these Jeeps for as little as $3.00 each, but there is a catch: at this price they must be purchased in lots of 50. The buyer is given so many days to strip the vehicles of parts, then the bodies and frames are crushed, and the buyer must have them removed.

Today's four wheel drive market offers something for everyone, from two-seaters, to roomy wagons, to nearly unstoppable offroad beasts.

ABOVE: *The Mitsubishi Shogun is one of the popular Japanese offerings in the 4×4 market in the United Kingdom.*

RIGHT: *The 1993 Range Rover is quite at home in the snows of Aspen, Colorado. Introduced in the U.K. in 1970, the Range Rover was a luxury offering from the Rover company in the U.K., which had put its first 4×4, the Land Rover, into production in 1948. The first U.S. specification Range Rovers went on sale in the U.S. in 1987.*

OPPOSITE TOP: *Made by AM General, the Hummer is certainly the toughest production 4×4 today. AM General can trace its roots back to the original Overland company.*

LEFT: *This cutaway of a 1993 Range Rover shows many internal details, such as the air suspension system, the 4.2 liter V-8 engine, and the 4WD mechanism.*

BELOW: *The Discovery by Land Rover has proven to be very popular in the British market.*

TRAIL RIDING

BY
JOHN D. FARQUHAR

TOP: *A row of 4×4s in the All Four Fun trail ride in the Colorado Rockies.*

OPPOSITE: *In moving down steep terrain, the vehicles stay spaced out for safety.*

From the highway, the mist-covered mountains, their quiet slopes thickly shrouded in timber, seem gentle and peacefully serene. From the road they look smooth, but up close they may well reveal some of the most rugged terrain ever to be challenged by man and machine. Nearly every owner of a four wheel drive has at one time or another wondered what it would be like to drive offroad. For some, just a few feet or perhaps miles is enough to satisfy their curiosity. But for others the art of trail riding is part of a lifestyle. What follows here is a profile of one of the better known trail rides in the United States. For information on other trail rides the reader is urged to contact associations listed in the directory in the back of this book.

For 20 years four wheelers have converged on the Cherokee National Forest for two weeks of intensive four wheel drive trail riding. The Great Smokey Mountain Venture is open to all four wheelers, whether they have offroad experience of not. Vehicles range from custom specialized trail rigs to stock Cherokees fitted with nothing more than heavily treaded tires. The organizers have divided the trails into four categories, ranging from easy to nearly impossible. Participants are urged to choose the category that best matches their level of experience and equipment.

The easiest is the Spare Film Run, a simple sightseeing tour that can be handled by stock vehicles. All a driver needs is spare film for his camera, and knowledge of how to read a map. The next rung up is the Spare Tire Run, a primer run for the less experienced and for stock vehicles. Drivers are urged to outfit their vehicles with rugged bias-ply, or the radial tires designed to resist severe sidewall abuse from sharp rocks and narrow, grating passages.

For the more adventurous there is the Spare Parts Run, intended for drivers already familiar with trail riding and who have their 4×4s well-prepared for the challenges that lay ahead. On this level of trails the driver must have an awareness of the dynamics of his vehicle in off-camber situations. Rollovers can happen, and paint and body damage is common for those that don't follow the

RIGHT: *In the Cherokee National Forest, some of the trails can be as easy as a dirt road, but what lurks beyond the next bend?*

BELOW: *This near show quality CJ, with its chrome wheels and bumpers, is not a common sight on trail rides, which are tough on vehicles.*

proper line over the trail. In addition to the tires, the entire driveline is prone to damage – this includes axles, hubs, pinion gears, and driveshafts. The best way to prevent damage is to prepare the vehicle thoroughly before leaving home, and to bring as many spare parts as possible. Ideally at this level the four wheeler would have a suspension lift, larger-than-stock tires, and a winch. Also recommended are underbody skidplates, a CB radio, tow straps, and a high lift jack.

The final category is the Spare Vehicle Run, the spare vehicle being a trailer, because hauling home may well be the only way to get the rig there. Locking differentials are added to the list of recom-

LEFT: *A stock CJ5 gets around "The Rock," a huge boulder that blocks the trail in the Smokey Mountain Venture.*

BELOW: *A four-cylinder 1984 Jeep Cherokee wagon crosses a stream in the Cherokee National Forest. Other than a four-inch lift and offroad tires, the vehicle is stock.*

mended vehicle improvements. Seat belts, a first-aid kit, rollcage, two spare tires, and a second, rear-mounted winch are also recommended. It is also advised to pack a large lunch, as the trail ride can last ten to twelve hours barring any problems. This top category offers even experienced offroaders the opportunity ot be part of a once in a lifetime adventure, and face the most demanding challenges that sanity permits.

After the first day the campgrounds are filled with the sounds of hammering and wrenching as vehicles are repaired for the next day. Many times by the second day some vehicles are mechanically unable to handle the tougher trails, and the four wheelers opt for scenery rather than the challenge of boulder-strewn trails and the winching of their 4×4s through narrow passages and dense woods. The four wheelers also do a lot of trail maintenance,

ABOVE: *It is important in offroading to prepare for anything, including sealing the electrical system to prevent water damage when crossing streams and lakes.*

RIGHT: *A Jeep covers some treacherous ground in the Sierra Trek, California. Sharp rocks and boulders can flatten tires, wreak havoc with the driveline, and cause serious underbody damage.*

OPPOSITE: *A Jeep pauses to solve a puzzle on a steep rocky face in Utah.*

ABOVE: *When traveling in mountain terrain, careful attention must be paid to the trail, as there are no guardrails.*

LEFT: *True offroad four wheeling gets the traveler into the scenery, not just gazing at it from the highway.*

OPPOSITE: *Jeeps scaling the Lion's Back, Moab, Utah.*

ABOVE: *Rugged trails can really test the suspension of even the most durable 4×4.*

RIGHT: *The driver must pay careful attention getting out of a tight spot, or he will ruin more than just his paint job.*

to protect the trails from washouts and other hazards. They also perform a lot of litter removal, and over the years have hauled out tons of trash and debris left by hikers and campers.

Trail riding in the National Forests is limited, and the Forest Service should be consulted before taking to the trails. Perhaps the best advice to a budding enthusiast is to join up with those that have already been there — if you break down, they'll get you out. There are two "nevers" in trail riding: Never trail ride alone, and never blaze a new trail. Newcomers to trail riding should be careful not to get in over their heads. They should take the easier trail, and get out of their vehicles and walk the trail to see what's up ahead; go slow, and take time to learn the trail. Once stuck, there are no towing services that will pull a four wheeler off a lonely mountain. Heed these words of wisdom from an experienced offroader: "Having four wheel drive means you can go fifty feet further in the mud than a two wheeler before you get stuck."

LEFT: *A Jeep scrambles up a steep rock grade in Moab, Utah.*

BELOW: *A Land Rover gets a helping hand on a trail. Trail guides provide assistance and direction on many organized trail rides.*

EXPEDITION VEHICLES

BY

GARY WESCOTT
*The Turtle
Expedition, Unltd.*

ABOVE: *An expedition on
the Oregon Trail brings The
Turtle Expedition to a
picturesque lake.*

To explore the vast and remote reaches of this planet, often far from civilization; to visit and experience countries and people seldom seen by the outside world; to travel overland to places never found in the brochures of your local travel agent. This is the essence of an expedition, and it is one of the most exciting uses for a sturdy four wheel drive vehicle.

The purpose of an expedition vehicle, simply stated, is to transport two or more individuals from point A to point B with *relative comfort, safety and reliability*, allowing the probability that point A and point B are separated by thousands of miles of dirt, mud and washboard roads pocked with enormous potholes, interrupted by unbridged rivers,

and inundated by extremes of weather.

There are some key points to focus on within this basic definition. "Relative comfort" is defined as that level of "roughing it" which you are willing to endure or are capable of enduring for the length of your expedition. If you enjoy sitting on the ground in the rain and swatting mosquitoes and no-see-ums while you eat beans out of a can, the preparation of your expedition vehicle can be greatly simplified.

If, at the other extreme, you require a real flush toilet and a hot shower at regular intervals, throwing a couple of sleeping bags and a cardboard box of supplies into the back of a VW bus will not be your cup of tea. If your budget allows, you may enquire about some of the English or German firms

ABOVE LEFT: *A dirt track in Wyoming yields breathtaking views of the Grand Tetons. Note the heavy towing bumper, an important improvement for an expedition vehicle.*

ABOVE: *A well-designed expedition 4×4 can bring you into the most spectacular scenery, such as these red rock cliffs in Utah.*

LEFT: *Gary Wescott relaxes after setting up a pop-up camper in a remote area of Moab, Utah. The Turtle 3 is a specially set-up Ford F350, and is diesel powered.*

who specialize in building custom 4×4 "motor homes" on the chassis of a Mercedes Unimog or a Man truck. Loaded with all the lastest refinements, including satellite phone and fax link-up, these rolling palaces can price out at over $3 million. There are many more affordable possibilities in between.

"Safety" should always be a consideration. It is closely tied to the specific destination of an expedition. If you're planning a year's drive around South America or across India, being able to cook your own food and filter your own water are certainly beneficial to the safety of your health. Protection from the elements, including disease-transmitting insects, is critical. It's also nice to know your vehicle is thief-proof enough to be where you parked it when you return from shopping in the market. Being stranded in a disabled truck hundreds of miles from nowhere might definitely jeopardize your safety. At the very least, it will ruin your day.

"Reliability" speaks for itself, though perhaps not loudly enough until it's too late. The import-

LEFT: *This Mercedes Unimog has been converted from an ambulance into a first class expedition vehicle to explore the wilds of South America.*

BELOW: *On a high altitude trip, snow and ice often require all fours to be locked in.*

ance of making sure the primary components such as brakes, tires, suspension, cooling system and drivetrain are in perfect condition *before* you begin an expedition cannot be overstated. Plan for all the necessary maintenance along the way, and give consideration to the availability of replacement parts throughout your destination.

Critical to the selection, design and preparation of an expedition vehicle is the knowledge of where you are going. If your intended route includes many long miles of sand or mud-choked jungle trails, weight will be your biggest problem. Tire selection is important, and some type of locking differentials will be very helpful. Too large or heavy a vehicle will severely limit where you can safely explore. Too small a camper will leave you tired, frustrated and travel-weary after only a few days on the road. The game rules are easy: How far off the beaten track can you get and still be comfortable when you turn off the engine?

In my 20 years of four wheel drive touring around the world, I have experienced everything from Land Rover Discoveries and 109s to fully prepared Unimogs. It has been my observation that 90 percent of the backroads in the world can be comfortably and safely negotiated in a standard American 4×4 pickup truck equipped with a slide-in camper. In fact, most roads have been made by this size vehicle.

A Ford F-350 one-ton 4×4 diesel-powered truck has been my choice for the past ten years. Equipped with Warn winches front and rear, BFGoodrich Mud-Terrain tires, and various other modest refinements, the Ford's reliability has been superb. I have passed through areas where even a slightly larger truck would have been stopped. The F-350 is capable of carrying the supplies and

ABOVE: *Gary Wescott's Turtle One straddles a monumental ditch on the road to Tikal, in Guatemala.*

RIGHT: *Turtle One climbs a steep grade in Baja California, Mexico. Note the spare tire on the hood.*

OPPOSITE: *The original Turtle sits in front of the Mayan temple at Tikal.*

amenities you need to enjoy your destination fully without exceeding its gross vehicle weight rating of about 9000 pounds. Fuel economy has been good. Diesel of reasonable quality can be found virtually anywhere, and Ford's international parts availability is excellent (the Ford F Series pickup is the single largest selling model of any vehicle in the world). Best of all, the American pickup, with some basic expedition modifications, is still in a price range affordable by the average would-be overland explorer. The huge selection of after-market products suitable for turning an American pickup into a specialized expedition vehicle, when compared to the task of custom fabrication, greatly reduces the expense and time of getting on the road to adventures.

The range of comfortable slide-in campers, new and used, which fit the bed of an American pickup is endless. I have attempted to build my own with limited success. In the end, the features and lightness of an aluminum-frame, factory-made camper are hard to duplicate for anything close to the same cost. The nine-foot Four-Wheel camper I have traveled in for several years has proven to be a strong and practical design. Features such as a comfortable bed, three-burner stove, heater and three-way refrigerator make it quite livable on cold, rainy nights. The pop-up feature greatly reduces wind drag, overall weight and top-heavi-

ABOVE: *A gigantic saguaro cactus dwarfs Turtle Three in America's desert Southwest. While the boat on top may seem a bit out of place in the desert, you never know what is around the next turn.*

RIGHT: *Four wheeling on a flooded old logging road in California. The 4×4 must be powerful enough to carry its load through such hazards. If it fails, then the winch comes in handy.*

ABOVE: *Turtle Three adds a motorbike to its preparations for adventure on and off the road.*

ness, all enemies of any vehicle used both on the highway and for backroad exploring. While American trucks and campers may not be available everywhere in the world, vehicles of similar size and weight should be given first choice.

A final word of advice: Be serious about preparing an expedition vehicle. If you plan to motel hop from city to city, a comfortable mid-sized sport utility vehicle such as the Ford Explorer, Land Rover Discovery, or Toyota Land Cruiser station wagon might be ideal, but don't try to live out of one. If you plan on exploring more remote areas where there are no hotels, you'll need the strength and weight-carrying ability of a full-size, partially self-contained truck and camper or the equivalent. Know where you're going and plan accordingly.

FOUR WHEELING AROUND THE WORLD

BY

GARY WESCOTT
*The Turtle
Expedition, Unltd.*

ABOVE: *Kicking back beside a secluded lake in the wilds of New Brunswick, Canada.*

The sport of four wheeling is truly international. From the boulder-strewn trails of California's High Sierras to the Green Lanes of England, and from the jungle and volcanic mountain passes of South America to the vast deserts of the Sahara, the Atacama and Australia's outback, virtually every country in the world has its four wheel drive enthusiasts.

In countries of high population density, four wheeling often takes the form of competitive trials in designated areas. These trials compress the most difficult parts of a month-long jungle adventure or an offroad race into a twisting maze of near-impossible hills and mug bogs marked out over an area no bigger than a couple of soccer fields. Such short courses are not limited to small countries. They are also popular in the United States, particu-larly on the East Coast. Stadium racing also has a large following.

In Colombia, for example, the largest 4×4 club in the country is called *Salta Montes* (The Grass-hoppers). Many of their 4×4s are built specifically for trial events. On any Sunday, you might find them at a local gravel quarry, testing their driving skill and their vehicle's limits. The predicaments they maneuver themselves into and out of are truly amazing.

Countries with more terrain to explore use it to good advantage. I once accompanied a group out of Quito, Ecuador, on an arduous trek into the nearby Andes. Mud and snow chains were necess-say, and winches were put to good use, as well as shovels and Hi-Lift jacks. The *aconcagua* mud was so slick, even walking on the flat was a challenge.

ABOVE AND LEFT: *In England the main offroading activity is "green laning" on public byways on private land.*

ABOVE: *The secluded beaches of Australia's Sunshine Coast can be reached by heavy duty tour bus or 4×4. Queensland's Teewah Coloured Sands features colorful sandstone cliffs backed by the Cooloola National Park.*

RIGHT: *A 4WD explorer in Australia encounters giant termite mounds 250 miles east of Darwin, in the Kakadu National Park.*

Australians with the proper equipment can roam across the vast Australian outback and not see more than a friendly kangaroo for days, though they have to be prepared to ford rivers and battle their share of talc-like bull dust and black earth, a deep gumbo of mud so deceiving, it can trap even the best drivers.

In countries such as Russia, Chile and Algeria — to mention only a few — there are trails that stretch for hundreds of miles into remote areas seldom explored. Even in the United States, some states, such as Nevada and New Mexico, offer abandoned desert two-tracks which may not have seen another vehicle for years. One summer several years ago, I drove a Land Rover across a portion of Nevada's Black Rock Desert. For an entire day we wound our way through sagebrush and across dry

ABOVE: *The rounded rocks of the Olgas are one of the many natural sights four wheelers can enjoy in the remote Northern Territory of Australia.*

LEFT: *For an expedition into South Australia's Flinders Ranges, the four wheeler must be sure his vehicle is well-prepared for the vast stretches of unpeopled land that characterize the Australian outback.*

43

arroyos with no sign of a road or trail. Under the current guidelines of Tread Lightly! and other conservation programs, such offroad exploring is becoming increasingly hard to find in the United States.

Perhaps more widely publicized are the international events involving many different countries. The most noted of these is the famed Camel Trophy, an annual four wheel drive adventure rally which draws its participants from as many as 16 nations. The Camel Trophy usually lasts two to three weeks and covers about 1000 miles traversing an area of jungle or mountains so difficult that locals laugh when you explain where the route is going. Other offroad events such as the annual Trans-Borneo run are also gaining in popularity, as much for their four wheeling difficulty as for the international camaraderie they offer to four wheelers from many walks of life.

In the true sense, most offroad races actually follow roads, so the name is misleading. And many of the entries for events such as the Paris-Dakar race or the granddaddy of offroad racing, the brutal Baja 1000 in Baja California, Mexico, are actually two-wheel drive. Nevertheless, the average four wheel drive vehicle would have difficulty negotiating these routes at normal speeds. The glamor and excitement of racing draws many spectators, some of whom use their four wheel drive vehicles to chase or support a race competitor, or just to gain a better vantage point from which to watch the race. Truth be known, without a pit crew waiting around the bend to fix what breaks, most offroad racers would never even finish. Something always breaks, even on a $250,000 race truck.

To explore with childlike curiosity, without preconceived notions: that is perhaps four wheeling at its finest. International four wheel drive touring is, in my own experience, the most exciting use of a 4×4. In the past 20 years exploring the backroads of the world, I have had my hubs locked in for a

ABOVE: *The Turtle encounters native huts in the barren mountains of Bolivia.*

FAR LEFT: *In Argentina some of the main roads in the back country are nothing more than gravel. The world traveler should do as much research as possible about what to expect at his destination before leaving home.*

LEFT: *The opportunity to see native animals, such as these llamas in Peru, is one of the great draws of four wheeling around the world.*

BELOW: *The only way to explore the Pacaya volcano in Guatemala is with all fours locked in.*

FOUR WHEELING

RIGHT: *In Brazil, the roads can be so bad that the only way through is to use cables and a winch.*

BELOW: *The world traveler can encounter all types of obstacles. This herd of cattle is blocking a muddy road in Colombia, South America.*

BOTTOM: *It always pays to find out what lies ahead and to plan accordingly. In Brazil, a washed-out bridge halted this expedition.*

month at a time. Often, four wheel drive may be used only five or six times a day, but without it, you may be forced to go back. Even on the worst of roads, four wheel drive will get you to that perfect camp at the high tide line, or right next to the river-bank.

The international scope of four wheel drive is not limited to the affluent. For the working man, it is simply a tool to get from point A to point B. The Colombian coffee merchant does not belong to a Jeep club (though there may be 50 flat-fender Jeeps in town), nor does the Mexican fisherman taking his catch of fresh lobster to town. His old 4×4 pickup is a necessity of life. For these and many others, there is no Camel Trophy, Jeeper's Jamboree or Paris-Dakar. Yet, they are every bit as much four wheelers as those who engage in it recreationally. Often, with far inferior equipment, they will nonchalantly drive places the recreational driver would eye with trepidation.

In the end, the simple fact of having traction to all four wheels is an amazing bond between men and women worldwide. That little "4×4" emblem is an international mark of madness. It says you'll leave the timid on the tarmac; that you'll dare to follow the road to its end, and you've got the right stuff to get you back. For work or play, that's four wheeling in any country of the world.

LEFT AND BELOW: *The Camel Trophy is one of the world's toughest offroad competitions. Each year 16 two-man teams are selected to compete. In the U.S. there is an average of 600 tryouts per year. Each team is given identical Land Rovers, and a series of tasks is set. Those who complete them first must go to the aid of others. The photographs on this page and on pages 48-49 are from the Camel Trophy in Madagascar in 1987.*

THESE PAGES: *Camel Trophy competitors must make their own trails, ford rivers, find their way over uncharted mountains, and right overturned vehicles. The routes chosen explore some of the harshest terrain in the most remote parts of the world. The Camel Trophy is, in many ways, the ultimate four wheeling experience.*

COMPETITION

BY

JOHN D. FARQUHAR and

BILL HOLDER

ABOVE: *X-Class four wheelers get the green light on the uphill drags at Gravelrama in Cleves, Ohio.*

Racing and other forms of four wheel drive competition began informally: Drag races began as friendly challenges to race across fields and meadows; hill climbs began with seeing whose Jeep could get to the top first; mud bogs started with the challenge of which vehicles could get through an extremely swampy, muddy stretch of trail. These informal races soon led to organized club events, but the rules and vehicle classifications varied from club to club, which caused a good bit of confusion for would-be competitors. Eventually the clubs formed associations, which provided a unified set of rules and classifications, and sanctioned events in different kinds of competition.

One of the leading racing associations in the United States is the East Coast Four Wheel Drive Association. Although it is also involved in land use and trail riding, promoting four wheel drive racing is one of its primary objectives. Many other groups have followed its lead in rules, classification of vehicles, and safety. Classes are based on weight-to-cubic-inch ratios, with add-on points for things like tires, nitrous oxide, blowers, and so on. Safety is of the utmost importance, with rollcages, engine and transmission shatter shields, six-point harnesses, and approved helmets being just some of the safety concerns.

In the beginning all vehicles competed in three to four events at any given race. The events included flat and uphill drags, hill climbs, and either timed or figure eight obstacle course racing. The program varied slightly from track to track. Over time, as the vehicles grew more specialized, they

became either drag machines or obstacle course racers, with some of both still competing on the hill climbs.

The drags are run on sand, gravel, or dirt, and the strip is 300 feet long. Most of the tracks have 700 feet or more of shut-down area for the bigger machines. The four wheelers are started with a traditional Christmas tree lighting system. The uphills vary in length from one track to another, but are similar to the flat drags. Everything from stock production vehicles to exotic open class four wheelers compete on the dragstrips.

The obstacle course competition is chiefly stock and slightly modified 4×4s. Two types of obstacle racing are run: timed and figure eight. The courses are similar in both, with jumps, tight turns, water hazards, and sometimes odd obstacles such as

ABOVE: *Faith Price in "Herbie" on the start of the uphill drags at Gravelrama. The only thing that is original on the CJ2A is the body.*

LEFT: *This long, lean four wheel drive sand racer is powered by over 400 cubic inches and given extra steam by a blower.*

giant teeter-totters. In the timed events a single vehicle is run at a time, with the run being clocked and the competitor with the fastest time winning his class. In the figure eight, two vehicles are run at a time, but they race in opposite directions along the track. The first to complete the entire course and return to the starting line wins the heat. The racing continues until there is a single winner in a class.

Hill climbs are judged by one of two factors: speed or distance. On small hill climbs the winner is usually the one with the fastest time over the top, while on the bigger hills the winner will be determined by who goes the farthest.

The largest four wheel drive offroad event in the United States is Gravelrama, produced by IOK 4-Wheelers of Cleves, Ohio. This East Coast-sanctioned event is held at the end of August each year, and draws an average of 400 competitors from 33 states and Canada for three days of intense offroad competition. One of the events that has made Gravelrama so popular is the Big Eliminator Hill Climb. This 170-foot mountain of pea gravel has defeated 85 percent of the vehicles that have attempted to crest it.

Short course wheel to wheel and desert racing also have a four wheel drive following, and are similar to obstacle racing other than that the competitors are all run at once. The events are dominated by dune buggies as well as two wheel drive trucks and cars. The short courses are usually set up so that the spectators can see all the action, with a set number of laps being run to determine

TOP: *A CJ5 comes out of the "Shark Pit" in the obstacle course competition at Gravelrama.*

ABOVE: *The Tri-County Four Wheelers of Lisbon, Ohio, offer something a bit different in obstacle racing: giant teeter-totters.*

RIGHT: *Wheel to wheel racing on a short course in Lake Geneva, Wisconsin.*

LEFT: *The Y-City Hill-toppers of Zanesville, Ohio, featured a steep hillclimb at their annual event.*

BELOW: *A Jeep pickup loses it just short of the top of the Big Eliminator at Gravelrama.*

ABOVE: *A four wheel drive truck plows through the sand at one of the longest and most brutal of desert races, the Baja 1000.*

RIGHT: *In desert racing, pit crews wait along the course to aid the competitors in repairs and refueling.*

5 4

the winners. Desert racing is done over open terrain, and varies in length from 200 to 500 miles. The pounding taken by the vehicles and crews is extreme, and at times winners are determined by who lasts the longest, as there are sometimes no finishers. Crashes, rollovers, and vehicles battered beyond repair are common in this type of competition.

Although popular, this type of racing does not lend itself well to four wheel drive. The 4×4s are heavier and stiffer than their two wheel drive counterparts, and the complexity of the four wheel drive mechanism makes them more prone to breakage, with the intensity and particular demands of this type of competition.

The drags, hill climbs, obstacle courses, and wheel to wheel racing are competitions of speed and, in some cases, endurance. Attention will now turn to two areas of four wheeling where raw power and brute strength are major factors in determining the winners: four wheel drive truck pulling, and mud bogging.

The sport of four wheel drive truck pulling comes from rural roots. It began with the popular two wheel drive trucks, but during the early 1980s some farm boys down in Kentucky decided to bring their stock 4WD trucks to a pull and ever since, pulling's never been the same.

The four wheel drive pulling portion of the sport has gained a great deal of support in the late 1980s and early 1990s and is now a popular part of the National Tractor Puller's Association (NTPA) national circuit. The 4WD trucks also participate with other pulling organizations, in some of which they top their powerplants with superchargers. In NTPA, the trucks are normally aspirated, but they can still make over 1000 horsepower.

These trucks retain their stock look, which most of the pullers feel is very important. A number of four wheel drive pullers like to use vintage bodies topping their machines, which the fans really love. They try to keep them as stock-appearing as possible. Also, these trucks must use the same brand of engine as the sheet metal on the outside. A Ford has got to be a Ford inside and out. Many fans have a favorite they like to root for.

Though they may look like stock trucks on the surface, they are full-race performance machines underneath. The frames are custom tube units often built of high-tech chrome moly steel.

One thing that really sets a 4WD pulling vehicle apart from other four wheelers is its weight. Unlike

BELOW: *The powerhouses of 4×4 competition are the pullers, which must have enough power to pull up to 90,000 pounds.*

other types of 4WD competition, the heavier the vehicle, the better. It's all a matter of acquiring traction, and weight is an important element. In NTPA competition there are two weight classes, 5800 and 6200 pounds. Much of the extra weight for these vehicles comes in the form of heavy steel weights which are hung on the nose of the vehicle. There is no suspension system on these vehicles — everything is solidly in place.

Special cleated tires are used to drive these awesome machines down the track. Their tall cleats have been cut down so that only a fine edge remains. With this type of tire cut, greater tire speed can be acquired and the truck can "hook" better to the track.

The final essential ingredient is, of course, a potent powertrain to put the horses to those four wheels. These are huge engines, up to 650 cubic inches in displacement, and sometimes greater. They are filled with high-performance internal parts built specifically for the tough job of pulling a many-thousand-pound sled. The strain on these engines is awesome, and once in a while they will fail under the load with a puff of smoke.

Since supercharging is not allowed on the NTPA national circuit, the chosen system is induction with exotic fuel injection systems. The power has

been quoted at as high as 1200 to 1400 horsepower for some of the top machines. All brands of powerplants, with all of the Big Three manufacturers represented, have had victories at one time or another. A lot of heavy-duty pieces must be employed in these powertrains, with ex-military parts being employed by many pullers.

Safety is a huge consideration in these trucks, with driveline looks and engine protection shields required. That way, an engine explosion would be contained and not pose a danger to the crowd.

With all the power available, it still all comes down to the driver himself to apply that power correctly. An understanding of track conditions is also important, because the texture of the track will have a great effect on the way the power should be applied. Most drivers, though, seem to come off the line slowly and then really punch the motor hard at about the 50-foot point. It's important to get up as much momentum as early as possible, since the weight on the hook is less early in the pull. As the truck progresses down the track, a weight box moves forward on the sled, transferring the weight to the front of the sled so that the truck is having to pull more and more of a dead weight. It's an exciting sport in which sheer power is the ultimate means to victory.

BELOW: *The spartan interior of a pulling truck sports a view of the massive powerplant.*

BELOW RIGHT: *Many pulling trucks have lift-up bodies to give quick access to the gigantic engines.*

While many pullers update their sheet metal every year some prefer the nostalgic look of the older trucks.

"Killer," a Florida-based puller, carries weights inside its huge front bumper to keep the front wheels down on the track.

ABOVE: *A stock class Ford Bronco attempts the mud pit at Sand-O-Rama, in Silver Lake, Michigan.*

Mud bogging, a natural for the 4×4s out-of-doors, has also been brought indoors with great success. A number of national organizations have included bogging as a part of their programs in recent years, with outstanding financial success. In some organizations, it is done in conjunction with pulling and other 4WD activities.

Without a doubt, mud racing is the dirtiest four wheel drive sport going. Viewing a driver and vehicle after a run in a particularly sloppy mud pit, there isn't a single square inch that isn't totally coated. Many shows have a clean-up area at the end of the track where everything can be hosed down.

At many mud shows, the fans are even brought into the action. Spectators are offered the chance to check out the goo themselves – not in a four wheeler, but on foot. Needless to say, a few of these contestants tend to get bogged down just like the vehicles.

There is no national sanctioning body for the four wheel mud sport – track construction is at the discretion of the event promotor. Outside tracks are obviously a lot longer than the inside variety, and as a result, end up being a lot faster. The indoor tracks, obviously constrained by the dimensions of the arena, are extremely small, and getting a rapidly accelerating machine stopped quickly is a serious consideration. Mudders have to start thinking about getting stopped before crossing the finish line. To encourage safety, many mud shows disqualify an entrant should he cross a certain line after completing his run. It is an exciting aspect of indoor mud racing when the vehicles try to negotiate a quick halt with muddy tires, causing them to skate.

Constructing an indoor track is not a pretty business. Thousands of cubic yards of dirt are hauled onto an arena floor and then fashioned into a challenging course with bulldozers and front end loaders. Since mud will be thrown everywhere, indoor show promoters frequently cover low sets with plastic sheets. Indoor mud tracks are usually about 100 feet long and up to 50 feet wide, with the actual "racing surface" two to four feet deep with mud. The gooey stuff usually has the consistency of freshly-poured cement, and for the competitors, it actually seems like concrete as it hardens up.

For outside events, the logistics of track-building are a lot easier: a pit is carved out, filled with mud, and then filled back in when the competition is completed. Outdoor tracks average around 300 feet in length.

As in 4WD truck pulling, the classes and rules for the vehicles vary, depending on the sanctioning body. There are usually two classes of vehicle: a modified class and an open class.

In many ways, mud bogging is really drag racing of a sort. As in drag racing, getting off the line at maximum RPMs is the key to success. But here, another key is to keep up the momentum and not let the mud bog you down.

In the open class, many of the vehicles use so-called paddle wheels, which have large cleats to do the "paddling." A successful Kentucky mudder explained that his technique involves coming off the line at about 5000 RPMs and then dropping into low gear. "If the engine picks up the revs, I shift it. If it bogs down, I leave it in low gear all the way through the mud," he explained.

The powerplants for mud vehicles are mostly Chevys and Fords, but there are a few Chrysler-powered machines. Every mudder has his own way of making power with carbs and fuel injection. The open class machines often employ nitrous power and supercharging.

One of the areas of four wheeling where two

forms of competition have been combined to create a new type of racing is mud drags. In this type of racing mud boggers and dragsters come together. The track is the standard 300 feet as in the drags, but instead of sand, the four wheelers race in about one foot of mud. The twist to this type of drag racing is that the wet, slippery mud can and often does throw the vehicle completely out of control. For the drivers it's a real challenge to maintain control while going as fast as they dare. The winners in this type of four wheel drive competition have to push their vehicles to the very limit of both speed and control.

Four wheel drive competition is some of the most exciting activity in motor sports today. Through cable television, more and more people have been exposed to the thrills of this type of racing. And as 4×4s become more popular with owners of motor vehicles, the interest in competition will be on the rise.

ABOVE: *Styled after the sand drag rigs, the newest class of mud bog vehicles can get enough RPMs to skim over the mud. They are usually judged on speed rather than on distance.*

LEFT: *Many of the early boggers were homebuilt rigs. Here, one goes down for the count in the pit.*

MONSTER TRUCKS

BY

*BILL
HOLDER*

ABOVE: *USA-1, owned and
driven by Everett Jasmer,
is perhaps the flagship of
the Chevy monster truck
fleet.*

OPPOSITE TOP: *Three
Predator 6000 carburetors
feed fuel to the massive
572 cubic inches of blown
Chevy powerplant in USA-1.*

OPPOSITE BOTTOM: *Bigfoot IX
sports a fiberglass body
and chrome moly frame.*

When they catapulted onto the motor sports scene in the 1980s, monster trucks were the hottest thing ever to hit the four wheel drive world. The giant machines, which often reach 12 feet in height and up to seven or eight tons in weight, have captured the imagination of young and old alike.

Initially, the giant four wheelers captivated admirers just with their size and appearance. Soon, the public demanded to see these trucks perform. The first monster truck maneuvers consisted of crawling over lines of junk cars. Eventually, the machines began competing against each other, and in recent years, the trucks have evolved from show vehicles to full-fledged racing vehicles. With advanced powerplants, greatly lightened chassis, and sophisticated suspension systems, these machines today are a far cry from their heavy, low-power predecessors.

In the early days, many monster trucks started

out with small block powerplants which could do some things, but were limited in other areas. It wasn't long before the switch was made to the big block powerplant. And even as the trucks continued to change and improve over the years, both Chevy and Ford big blocks have continued to stay on the motor mounts.

All of the competitive monster trucks use superchargers coupled with carburetors for making their fire, but there are others that use fuel injection, with and without supercharging, for their purposes. There are also those which use carburetors by themselves. Others get their power from a nitrous bottle that can whip on an additional hundreds of horsepower for a short burst, which is what is often needed with these monster machines. Availability of funds plays a big part in the selection of power for the monster trucks.

Over the years, Chevy powerplants have probably been the most popular of the engines. Ready

availability of parts is probably the biggest reason for this selection. There are also a lot of Ford-powered monster trucks, including Bob Chandler's Bigfoot fleet.

Though few and far between, a few trucks have worn the Chrysler Pentastar emblem. Thus far, there have been no foreign powerplants in this All-American sport.

But no matter how great the power under the hood, it is of no value unless there is an effective four wheel drive powertrain to get those hundreds of horsepower to those tall tires. Many of the trucks use transmissions which are the same brand as the powerplant. Most of the Chevy-powered trucks use beefed-up versions of the

ABOVE: *A 464 cubic inch supercharged Ford big block engine powers Larry Tura's Hercules.*

ABOVE RIGHT: *A good suspension system is one of the keys to a winning monster truck. Note the shock and spring combination shown here, which gives the truck a lot of cushion on landings.*

Turbo 400, while many Fords have modified C-6 transmissions. Most builders also equip their transmissions with racing torque converters which allow the enigne to rev up to its power range before transmission lock-up. Other trucks use custom-built transmissions, such as a two-speed Lenco airshift.

Initial transfer cases for the monsters were ex-military equipment, and the trend continues today. The heavy gearing allows the unit to handle the heavy stresses from the huge engine power. But as was true with the transmissions, there are those builders who have stepped beyond and built strictly custom units for their particular needs. The driveshafts must deal with awesome loads, and again, ex-military equipment still serves in many of these unique trucks.

The final pieces in this complex puzzle of parts are the front and rear differentials. Most of the builders use differentials equipped with super-strong planetary gears. Trucks have broken differentials in the past, and have made luckless

attempts to go it with just the front or rear set of wheels driving. It takes a lot to drive a set of these tires, each weighing about 1000 pounds. A vast majority of the monster truck teams use 66-inch diameter tires. There are those, however, that don't like to conform. The Bigfoot V, for example, uses an amazing set of 120 inch tires.

As monster truck design has matured over the years, the importance of an effective suspension system has become a major concern. Suspension technology has advanced tremendously over the past decade. When the monster craze first started in the late 1970s, the trucks were just basically jacked up on their existing suspension systems. They were not capable of doing much more than just supporting the weight of the trucks. It was obvious that if the trucks were to perform and compete, something had to be done.

One driver recalled that the original suspension systems were big and heavy, just like the trucks themselves. Nothing moved and many of the

LEFT: *Hercules shows off its special lift-up body.*

LEFT: *This unique monster truck is equipped with suspension from a Corsair A7 jet.*

trucks had eight, and sometimes as many as ten, shocks on each corner of the truck. There are a lot fewer shocks on today's trucks, and shocks are light and spongy, to provide as much give as possible. With the sky-high jumps that the trucks are now making, there needs to be as much absorption on impact as possible in order to save the driver's body. Many drivers are also using special form-fitting racing seats and belts to help take up the shock.

Some of the new monster trucks have demonstrated almost two feet of suspension depression. One problem that the monster builders are facing with the soft suspension, however, is due to the big power of the engines. The torque, with the soft suspension, can actually twist the front end of the truck – a strange sight to behold.

As with other components of the monster trucks, the frame design is also being directed by race car technology, with steel tube frames now appearing. These designs are lighter and stronger than in the past, and greatly aid in the goal to lighten up these trucks. The rollcage is extremely important for driver safety, since these five to ten ton trucks do go over at times.

OPPOSITE: *Bigfoot V in a mud bog at the Indianapolis 4-Wheel and Offroad Jamboree. The only truck to sport 10-foot tires, Bigfoot is the tallest and perhaps the heaviest of all monster trucks.*

LEFT: *The four link suspension system is now used throughout monster truck competition. It allows up to 24 inches of travel.*

BELOW: *The name of Bob Fisher's Ford Liquidator promotes the owner's full-time business and suggests to fans that it means to "liquidate" the competition.*

Steering these trucks is a heavy requirement for these giant machines. With all four wheels driving, it's necessary to be able to steer all of them, hence the trucks have independent steering on both the front and rear. This arrangement enables some of the trucks actually to turn within their own lengths. It's also quite a sight to see one of these trucks coming straight at you with the body cocked at a different angle.

Getting one of these machines up to 60 miles per hour is one thing, but getting it stopped quickly is quite another. This used to be accomplished by brakes on all four wheels, but the trucks now use a driveline brake, where stopping power in the form of a standard brake assembly is applied directly to the driveline.

In competition, the monsters also have a radio unit on board that can receive a signal from the sidelines to shut down the engine and stop the machine. Safety is a big consideration with the monster trucks, and the sanctioning bodies are working hard to ensure that it stays that way.

The most visible characteristic of the monster trucks is the colorful body sitting high up in the sky. One might think that the bodies would be highly modified to go along with the obviously modified undercarriages. Some bodies are changed, but for the most part the trucks carry stock sheet metal.

In many cases, the trucks try to keep up with the sheet metal of the latest model year. The car companies are obviously using some of these trucks as advertising tools. They might not look like the

RIGHT: *Gary Bauer's Ford Lon Ranger is one of the few short wheelbase trucks still in competition today.*

BELOW: *At the IOK 4-Wheelers grounds in Cleves, Ohio, Bigfoot and Nitemare face off in the uphill drags.*

trucks you can buy in the showroom, but even still there is a lot of fan recognition.

Glistening engines and snappy paint jobs attract a lot of attention from the fans. The paint jobs on many of the trucks are of show car quality, but it's not easy to keep them looking nice. The shiny coatings of paint get rubbed, dirty, scratched, and sometimes, totally smashed. On occasion, it's necessary to completely reskin one of these monsters after a crash.

Some monster truck teams have a sponsor to help with the expenses, and as a result the sponsor's colors dominate the paint scheme of the trucks. The USA-1 team has an agreement with the True Value Hardware Company, as does Bigfoot with the Ford Motor Company.

In a class of their own, monster trucks are a colorful and unusual aspect of the 4WD world.

ABOVE: *Corporate sponsors often provide big money to monster truck teams in exchange for highly visible advertising space. Here, Mattel Toys promotes its Hot Wheels miniature cars as part of Bigfoot's glistening paint job.*

RIGHT: *For monster truck racing, tires are cut to give better traction and to lower the weight.*

OPPOSITE: *Shiny paint and eye-catching graphics are used to make each truck stand out. Note how the fenders on Monster Patrol are cut out to clear the huge tires.*

OPPOSITE INSET: *Wildfoot, a new addition to the Bigfoot fleet.*

SHOW AND SHINE

BY

JOHN D.
FARQUHAR

They sit in rows, their bright chrome glistening in the sun. Their custom-painted hues vary from very bright, to very graphic, to dark, and no two are alike. They seem all to feature incredible workmanship, from the paint, to the custom drivelines, to the engines with each powerplant built and tuned to give the maximum amount of horsepower possible. They all sit on the finest offroad tires available. Yet they seldom if ever go offroad, for they are four wheel drive show trucks.

Most owners state that they drive the custom show rigs to the shows, although some trailer theirs in. A few admit they drive the handsome four wheelers on a daily basis. But almost to a man they confess they do not do any offroading in these pristine, customized vehicles.

Most of the flashy show 4×4s begin either as stock vehicles being restored or wrecked trucks being rebuilt. Turning a production rig into a show quality 4×4 can run from a couple of thousand to one hundred thousand dollars or more. It all depends on what the owner wants, and what he or she can afford.

Much attention is given to paint and design. Some of the trucks sport custom colors layered on up to twenty coats, each hand rubbed, until they look deep enough to dive into. Many sport hand-painted graphics and murals done to painstaking

OPPOSITE: *Custom paint is perhaps the biggest factor in what makes show 4×4s special. Many layers of paint, each one of which is hand rubbed, give the custom color glistening depth.*

LEFT: *A show class Jeep, fitted with special chrome and lights and sporting a custom paint job.*

ABOVE: *The latest high-tech computer designed graphics adorn this Ford.*

RIGHT: *A show class vintage Ford Bronco. Note the tie-in of underbody paint and components such as wheel rims to chassis colors.*

detail and perfection. The hottest thing in design on today's trucks are computer printed graphics — special labels laser-printed to the owner's custom order — and no two are alike. It can even be difficult for an owner to reproduce his own design should the original be damaged.

Other items are considered in the design, such as light kits, steps, wipers, upholstery, dash, and so on.

Careful attention is also paid to engineering details. Front and rear ends are replaced by stronger-than-stock after-market parts. Engines are often torn down and rebored to gain more cubic inches. All the part are polished until they gleam, and in the rebuild are often topped off with blowers or performance carbs. Some builders even color match the wiring and spark plug wires to the color of the truck. Most of the owners hope

ABOVE: *Something different: a Chevy 2WD El Camino converted into a four wheeler.*

LEFT: *A real show stopper, this Chevy powerplant is carefully detailed.*

OPPOSITE: *Chromed and blown: a customized show engine.*

ABOVE AND LEFT: *The Thriller features neon graphics that make it a standout. Unlike many show 4×4s, it is driven daily.*

that their trucks will be picked to appear in one of the popular four wheel drive magazines, so paying attention to detail can often really pay off.

The biggest of the four wheel drive shows are the series of 4-Wheel and Off-Road Jamborees, produced by Special Events of Indianapolis, Indiana. The Jamborees also feature monster truck races, mud bogging, and more. Each show also features a commercial row, selling parts and custom add-ons, and even custom painting.

As we have seen in the pages of this book, four wheeling offers motorists an unequalled degree of freedom and excitement. On and off the road, there is truly nothing quite like being behind the wheel of a four wheeler.

BELOW: *"Denny Did It" offers custom painting at many Jamborees and show competitions. The events can draw up to 2000 competitors on a weekend, and thousands of spectators.*

RIGHT: *One-of-a-kind computer-age graphics on a show 4×4. Should the vehicle be damaged, the graphics would be nearly impossible to reproduce.*

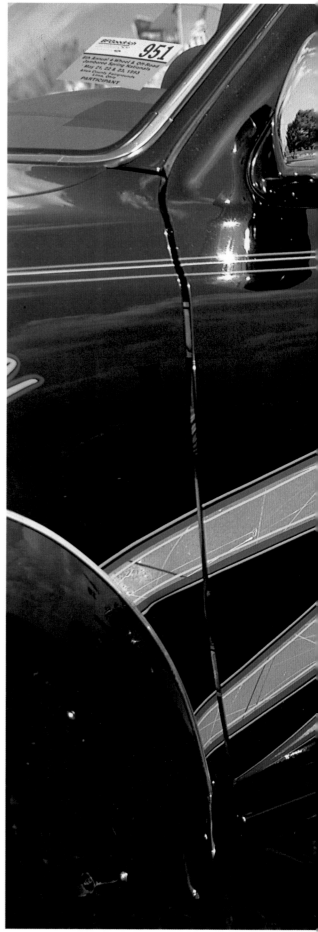

DIRECTORY

NORTH AMERICAN ASSOCIATIONS
Arizona State Association of Four Wheel Drive Clubs
P.O. Box 23904, Tempe, AZ 85282

Associated Blazers of California
P.O. Box 1432, Norwalk, CA 90650

California Association of 4WD Clubs
3104 "O" St. #313, Sacramento, CA 95816

Colorado Association of 4WD Clubs
P.O. Box 1413, Wheat Ridge, CO 80034

East Coast 4WD Association
101 S. Miami Ave. Cleves, OH 45002

Four Wheel Drive Association of British Columbia
24967 122 Ave, Maple Ridge, BC, Canada
V4R 1Z8

Great Lakes 4WD Association
928 Clyde, Owasso, MI 48867

Indiana 4WD Association
6142 Franklin Rd., Hagertown, IN 47346

Kentucky 4WD Association
101 Lakeshore Dr., Hardinsburg, KY 40143

Mid-America 4WD Association
2316 Prospect, Springfield, MO 65803

Mid West 4WD Association
2410 N.W. 15½ St., Faribault, MN 55021-3425

Montana 4×4 Association
111 7th Ave. W., Polson, MT 59860

Pacific Northwest 4WD Association
948 18th, Longview, WA 98632

Southern 4WD Association
1249 Robert Lane NE, Marietta, GA 30062

Southwest 4WD Association
5500 Sweetwater NW, Albuquerque, NM 87120

Tread Lightly!, Inc.
298 24th Street, Suite 325-C, Ogden, UT 84401

United Four Wheel Drive Association
4505 W. 700 S. Shelbyville, IN 46176

Utah 4WD Association
P.O. Box 20310, Salt Lake City, UT 84120

Virginia 4WD Association
P.O. Box 722, Mechanicsville, VA 23111

Wisconsin 4WD Association
203 Gruenwald Ave., Neenah, WI 54956

INTERNATIONAL ASSOCIATIONS
All Wheel Drive Club
c/o Peter Facey, 134 Sandyhurst Lane, Ashford, Kent, United Kingdom, TN25 4NT

Australia National Four Wheel Drive Clubs
c/o Brian Tanner, 28 Drysdale Ave., Hamlyn Heights, 3215 Victoria, Australia

South Africa Jeep Club
P.O. Box 28354, Sunnyside 0132, South Africa

OPPOSITE: *The four wheeler's creed: Take with you only your memories, and leave nothing but your tracks.*

INDEX

Numbers in *italics* indicate illustrations

Acknowledgments

The authors would like to thank their wives, Ruthanne, Monika, and Lorraine, for their patience and support on this project.

Thanks also go to the following individuals and organizations for their assistance:
East Coast 4 Wheel Drive Association, its clubs and members.
Special Events and Susan Davis, Indianapolis, IN
National Tractor Pulling Association, Worthington, OH
Monster Truck Racing Association, Hazelwood, MO
Bob Chandler-Bigfoot Inc. Hazelwood, MO
Army Armstrong
2/174 ADA Hawk unit, U.S. Army
Armed Forces Day Committee, Findlay, OH
Great Lakes Four Wheel Drive Association
Great Smokey Mountain Venture/Tom Hoskins
Pro-Shows, Kentucky

All photography was provided by John D. Farquhar and Gary and Monika Wescott except for the following:
AM General Corporation: page 20(top).
Australian Picture Library: page 42(both).
Nick Dimbleby: page 41(both).
Jeep/Eagle: page 18(bottom).
Land Rover North America: pages 7, 20(bottom), 21(top).
Andrew Moreland: page 20(center).
National Motor Museum, Beaulieu: page 21(bottom).
Weldon Trannies: page 43(both).